Eva
the Afro - Latina

Eva Sarai Johnson

Are you wondering what Afro-Latina means?

My dad's skin is brown and my mom's skin is peach.

My skin is actually tan.

A perfect mixture of my mom and my dad.

My hair is curly, brown and healthy.

My dad is African American.

My dad's family speaks English.

Together, we celebrate our differences.

Differences are what makes us special.

I have the best of both worlds.

THE END

Now it's your turn!
What do you love about your culture?

Draw a picture of the flag that represents your culture:

What do you love about yourself?

_____

_____

_____

_____

_____

_____

_____

Draw a picture of your family:

Made in United States
North Haven, CT
28 April 2023

35953916R00015